Modern Industrial World

Germany

Patrick Burke

Wayland

MODERN INDUSTRIAL WORLD

Austria

Benelux Countries

Canada

France

Germany

Ireland

Israel

Italy

Japan

Portugal

Russia

South Africa

Spain

Sweden

Cover: Modern art outside the Europa Centre in the heart of Berlin.
Contents page: Coffee, cakes and ice-cream at the famous Kranzler cafe on Berlin's Kurfürstendamm.

Series editor: Paul Mason
Series designer: Malcolm Walker
Editorial management: Serpentine Editorial

First published in 1995 by
Wayland (Publishers) Ltd
61 Western Road, Hove
East Sussex, BN3 1JD, England

British Library Cataloguing in Publication Data
Burke, Patrick
 Germany. – (Modern Industrial World Series)
 I. Title II. Series
 943.08

ISBN 0–7502–0985–2

Typeset by Kudos Design
Printed and bound by G. Canale & C.s.p.A, Turin, Italy

Contents

Introduction

Germany, whose full name is the Federal Republic of Germany, lies at the heart of Central Europe. It has a small northern coastline and shares frontiers with nine countries: Denmark to the north; the Netherlands, Belgium, Luxembourg and France to the west; Switzerland and Austria to the south; and the Czech Republic and Poland to the east.

Of the 90 million German speakers in Central Europe, almost 9 out of 10 live in Germany. The rest are in Austria, Switzerland, Italy, and parts of Belgium, France and Luxembourg. There are also some German-speaking minorities in Poland, Romania and the former Soviet Union. After Russia, Germany is the most populous country in Europe.

Looking west from the Kurfürstendamm at the Kaiser-Wilhelm Memorial Church. The church, built in the 1890s, was almost completely destroyed in the Second World War. It is now a war memorial and a major Berlin landmark.

DENMARK

BALTIC SEA

NORTH
SEA

Kiel
SCHESWIG
HOLSTEIN

P
O
L
A
N
D

Hamburg

Elbe

Bremen

LOWER SAXONY

Berlin

N
E
T
H
E
R
L
A
N
D
S

Weser

Hanover

NORTH RHINE
WESTPHALIA

GERMANY

Leipzig

Düsseldorf

Dresden

Cologne

Rhine

BELGIUM

RHINELAND
PALATINATE

Frankfurt

Main

CZECH REPUBLIC

LUXEMBOURG

Neckar

B A V A R I A

Danube

F
R
A
N
C
E

Stuttgart

BADEN WÜRTTEMBURG

AUSTRIA

Munich

SWITZERLAND

LIECHTENSTEIN

0	50	100	150	200	250 km

0	50	100	150 miles

LANDSCAPE

Germany has a rich and varied landscape, ranging from the Alps and the Alpine foothills in the south, through the Central German Uplands, to the North German Plain.

Only a small part of the Alps is in Germany - in Bavaria, where the country borders on Austria (the rest are in France, Switzerland, Austria and Italy). From the Alps, the wide hilly Alpine foothills, with their moors and lakes, slope down gradually to the River Danube.

The Central Uplands divide north Germany from the south. With its rolling hills and forests, this is one of the prettiest parts of the country. The Black Forest in the south-west, the Hunsrück and Eifel hill ranges in the west, and the higher Harz Mountains in the centre are very popular with hikers.

In the northern parts of Germany there are heaths and moors, and flat plains dotted with lakes. The Baltic coast has sandy beaches. Rügen, a favourite holiday centre, is separated from the mainland by a narrow channel.

Neuschwanstein castle, built by the 'fairytale king' Ludwig II of Bavaria in the nineteenth century. Behind is the Alpsee, one of the many lakes in the Bavarian Alps.

CLIMATE

In the Alps and the Central Uplands, spring comes late, followed by a short, hot summer and a long cold winter. In the northern lowlands and on the coast, the seasons are less extreme: winter is milder and summer is cooler. The Harz Mountains have their own climatic zone, with cold winds, a cool summer and heavy snow in the winter.

Though not as high as the Alps, the mountains are very popular with skiers. In Upper Bavaria, the dry, warm wind called the Föhn blows down from the Alps.

CLIMATE			
	January	July	Rainfall
Alps	-4 °C	20 °C	100 cm
Northern Lowlands	-2 to 0 °C	16-18 °C	60 cm
Harz Mountains	-4 °C	16 °C	80 -100 cm

6

RIVERS

The Rhine is the longest river in Germany and the most important industrial waterway in Europe. Barges carry goods along it between Rotterdam in the Netherlands and Basel in Switzerland. The Rhine runs through some of the most beautiful countryside in Germany, with vineyards on both sides and picturesque castles overlooking the river. In the east, German's second-longest river, the Elbe, rises in the Czech Republic and enters the sea at Hamburg.

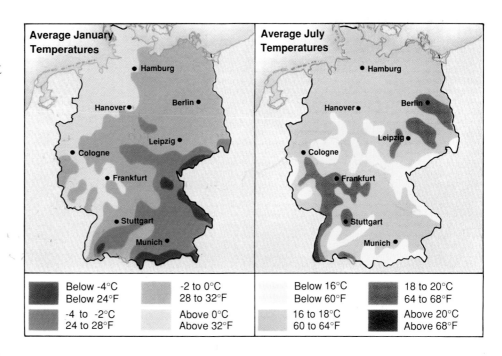

Average January Temperatures

Average July Temperatures

Below -4°C / Below 24°F	-2 to 0°C / 28 to 32°F
-4 to -2°C / 24 to 28°F	Above 0°C / Above 32°F

Below 16°C / Below 60°F	18 to 20°C / 64 to 68°F
16 to 18°C / 60 to 64°F	Above 20°C / Above 68°F

Average January and July temperatures.

GERMANY AT A GLANCE

Area: 357,000 square kilometres.

Population: 79.9 million (64 million in former West Germany; 15.9 million in the former German Democratic Republic; 5.9 million foreign nationals).

Population density: 222 people per square kilometre.

Capital: Berlin.

Languages: German; Turkish; Sorb.

Religions: Christianity; Islam.

Minorities: Sorbs approx. 60,000; Danes (in Schleswig) approx. 30,000; Sinti and Roma (gypsies) approx. 30,000.

Currency: Deutschmark (DM).

Highest mountain: Zugspitze (2962 metres).

Longest river: Rhine (865 kilometres inside Germany).

The Rhine and the dramatic country of its river valley. This part of Germany has inspired poets and produced many legends.

History

For over a thousand years before 1871 Germany was not a single country but a collection of different-sized states. These states were governed under separate rulers and occasionally fought bloody wars with each other. In theory, the supreme authority in the German lands was the Holy Roman Empire, founded by the Emperor Charlemagne in 800 AD (and finally abolished by the French Emperor Napoleon in 1806). But for most of its existence the Empire had little power.

In 1517, an obscure monk called Martin Luther sparked off a religious revolution which produced a new branch of Christianity known as Protestantism. A hundred years of religious conflict followed between Protestantism and the Roman Catholicism, ending in the terrible Thirty Years War (1618-48) which destroyed parts of Germany. In the late 1600s Prussia emerged as a strong state and by the late 1700s was a major European power.

Charlemagne (above) was crowned Emperor by the Pope in recognition of the wars he fought against the enemies of Christian Europe.

THE SECOND REICH

In 1871 a unified Germany – the Second Empire, or Reich – was created under the leadership of Prussia, with Otto von Bismarck as chancellor.

Between 1871 and 1914, Germany became one of Europe's leading industrial nations. Abroad, it increasingly pursued an aggressive foreign policy which culminated eventually in the outbreak of the First World War in 1914.

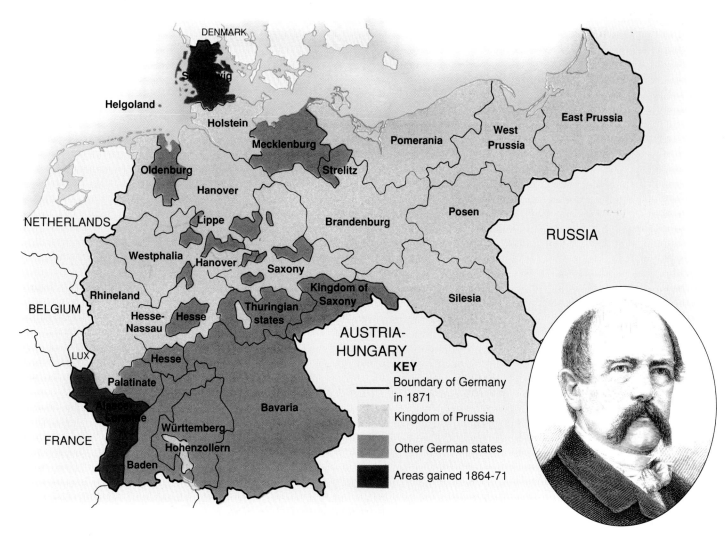

KEY
Boundary of Germany in 1871
Kingdom of Prussia
Other German states
Areas gained 1864-71

German unification was completed in 1871 under the leadership of Otto von Bismarck, prime minister of Prussia. By manoeuvering the German states to fight three wars (against Denmark, Austria and France) Bismarck unified them to form the German Empire.

WEIMAR

Defeat in the war in 1918 brought down the German Emperor. A democratic state was established, known as the Weimar Republic after the town where its constitution was drawn up.

The Weimar period was a time of great economic and political instability. Many Germans rejected parliamentary democracy and the Republic was subjected to constant attacks from left and right-wing groups. The most successful of these was the far-right Nazi Party of Adolf Hitler. He came to power in 1933 and replaced the democratic state with a one-party dictatorship which was called the Third Reich.

Bismarck (above) was known as the 'Iron Chancellor'. He became prime minister of Prussia in 1862 and outlined his policy in the famous phrase: 'The great issues of the day will not be settled by speeches and the resolutions of majorities [in parliament] but by blood and iron.'

1871   Germany is unified. Beginning of Second Reich.

1914   First World War begins. Germany allied with Austria–Hungary against Britain, France and Russia.

1918   Germany and Austria–Hungary defeated.

1919   Weimar Republic established.

1933   Adolf Hitler becomes chancellor. End of Weimar Republic. Germany becomes one-party state under Hitler's National Socialist German Workers' (Nazi) Party. Beginning of the Third Reich.

1939   Germany invades Poland. Second World War begins.

1945   Germany surrenders to the Allies and is occupied by their forces.

1949   Federal Republic of Germany founded in May. German Democratic Republic founded in October.

1955   West Germany joins NATO. Warsaw Pact formed.

1958   EEC (European Economic Community) comes into being, with France, West Germany, Italy, the Netherlands, Belgium and Luxembourg as members.

1961   Berlin Wall erected on 13 August.

1969   SDP and FDP form new government with Willy Brandt as chancellor.

1972   West Germany and the GDR sign the Basic Treaty.

1985   Mikhail Gorbachev comes to power in the Soviet Union and starts reform process.

1989   Hungary dismantles border with West. Thousands of East Germans leave for West Germany. Movement for democratic change in GDR. East German Communist Party loses its leading role and the Berlin Wall is opened.

1990   Germany is reunified.

Millions of East Germans visited West Germany after the border was opened on 9 November 1989. Here a queue of Trabants waits to cross the border.

THE NAZI PERIOD

In the early years of Nazi rule, the economy improved considerably. The Nazis started projects that helped bring down unemployment, for example building motorways. But there was a much darker side to their rule. The Nazis

Adolf Hitler, who gave himself the name of Führer, taking the salute at the German Labour Service parade during a Nazi Party rally in Nuremberg.

banned other political parties and arrested anyone who publicly disagreed with them. They built concentration camps, in which Jews, Gypsies, political opponents, homosexuals and disabled people were imprisoned, tortured and murdered.

In 1939 Germany went to war again. In the Second World War Germany was defeated by the combined might of allied Soviet, American and British forces. By the time the war ended in 1945 about 10 million people had been killed in concentration camps. Perhaps 6 million were Jews, and with them were most of Europe's Gypsies.

The eagle emblem on the coat of arms has been used in Germany since the ancient Romans introduced it.

THE TWO GERMANIES

After the Second World War, Europe and Germany were divided. The Soviet Union dominated the countries it had liberated from the Nazis. Like the Soviet Union, they

Willy Brandt and Ostpolitik

In October 1969 Willy Brandt became chancellor of West Germany at the head of a coalition government of the Social Democratic Party (SDP) and the Free Democratic Party (FDP). Brandt was mayor of West Berlin when the Berlin Wall was built in 1961. He decided it was important for there to be dialogue and closer political relations between West Germany and the communist countries of Eastern Europe, rather than confrontation. As chancellor he pursued this Ostpolitik energetically. West Germany signed treaties that improved relations with the Soviet Union and Poland. In 1972 the two Germanies signed the Basic Treaty, in which they recognized each other's sovereignty.

Some people opposed Ostpolitik because they said it gave away too much to the communist countries. But many supported it because it helped to ease tensions between East and West. Without weakening West Germany's ties to the West, Willy Brandt's Ostpolitik helped make the Cold War less dangerous.

became one-party states with centralized economies, and members of the communist economic bloc, COMECON, and of the Soviet-led military alliance, the Warsaw Pact. The eastern part of conquered Germany, occupied by Soviet troops, became the German Democratic Republic (GDR), or East Germany.

The countries of Western Europe allied themselves to the United States. They became parliamentary democracies, developed market economies and joined the European Economic Community and the West's military alliance,

Willy Brandt (above) was one of only two Social Democratic chancellors in post-Second World War West Germany (the other was Helmut Schmidt).

NATO. Western Germany, occupied by the Americans, the British and the French, became the Federal Republic of Germany, or West Germany.

From 1945 until 1989 relations between the two halves of Europe, and the United States and the Soviet Union, were strained. This period was known as the Cold War.

The West German economy grew quickly and remained powerful. By the end of the 1980s it was the world's third strongest. The East German economy was weaker, but by the 1980s it was ranked the world's tenth strongest and East Germans enjoyed the highest standard of living in the Eastern bloc.

The reforms of Mikhail Gorbachev in the Soviet Union in the 1980s, however, weakened the position of communist governments in Eastern Europe. East Germans, like others, became bolder in demanding change. In the autumn of 1989 they launched a peaceful revolution that overthrew the government and paved the way for German unification. This, with similar revolutions in other Eastern European communist states, brought the division of Europe and the Cold War to an end.

An East German workman repairing a hole in the Berlin Wall caused by an explosion in May 1962. Over the years the western side of the Wall in central Berlin became covered in graffiti, slogans and paintings.

The two Germanies, 1949-1990.

The East German Revolution of 1989

Throughout 1989 Hungary gradually dismantled its wire-fence border with Austria. The revolution began in September, when thousands of East Germans began to cross the border to get to West Germany. In the GDR, opposition groups were founded, including New Forum and Democracy Now. Demonstrations for reforms became even larger; on 4 November 1989 one million people gathered in East Berlin.

Many people who lived in East Germany wanted a Western standard of living, which they saw every day on West German TV.

Others wanted to keep the GDR socialist, but make it more democratic. All of them wanted political freedoms and the freedom to travel. The turning point came on 9 November, when the East German government opened the border between the two Germanies. From now on the demands for unification were louder than those for reform.

Throughout 1990 the momentum towards unification speeded up. On 3 October, less than a year after the Berlin Wall had been opened, the two countries were united.

Before 9 November demonstrators in Leipzig called for the reform of East Germany. After the Berlin Wall came down they demanded unification with West Germany.

Berlin

The Brandenburg Gate, built for King Frederick William of Prussia in the eighteenth century, is one of Berlin's most famous landmarks. The four-horse chariot, or Quadriga, on top holds the symbol of victory.

Berlin in ruins after the Second World War. In the early years after the Second World War women known as Trümmerfrauen (women of the rubble) worked in teams to clear away rubble and rebuild the city.

Berlin's origins lie in the twelfth century, when two trading towns, Berlin and Cölln, were established on the river Spree. In the seventeenth century, after 500 years as a trading city, it began to produce goods of its own.

By the nineteenth century, Berlin was well-known for its heavy machinery and machine tools, electrical and chemical products, fine textiles and porcelain. Industrialization brought population increase: from 150,000 in 1786 to 1.9 million by 1890.

In 1871 Berlin became the capital of a united Germany and remained so until 1945. In the 1920s and 1930s, the city was Germany's cultural centre, where famous people such as the playwright Bertolt Brecht lived and worked. In the Second World War, Berlin was devastated by bombing and ground battles. By the end of the war in May 1945, huge sections of the city were in ruins, with only one out of every three buildings left intact.

AFTER THE SECOND WORLD WAR

By 1949 Berlin had been divided into two parts. The eastern part became capital of the German Democratic Republic (GDR). The western part was a capitalist 'island' surrounded by the GDR, and could only be reached from West Germany along road, rail, or air corridors, or canals. Legally, West Berlin was never fully part of West Germany. The mayor and elected government largely ran the city, but it was 'occupied' by the Allies from the end of the Second World War. It also depended heavily on subsidies from West Germany.

For the next forty years divided Berlin was a symbol of the Cold War. On many occasions, it was a flashpoint in the relations between East and West, for example in August 1961 when the East German government built the Berlin Wall.

The Marienkirche in east Berlin is the city's oldest surviving parish church (it is first mentioned in records in 1294). It faces on to Karl Liebknecht street, named after the socialist revolutionary leader.

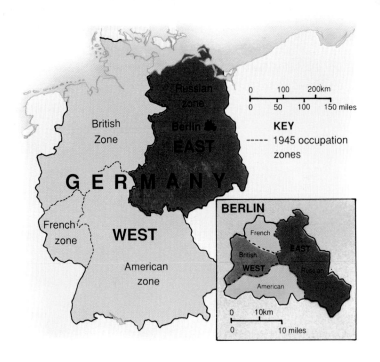

Berlin between 1945 and 1990, when it was under the ultimate control of the four victors in the Second World War (France, the UK, the Soviet Union and the USA), each of which had its own sector.

'German greatness and German megalomania – Berlin played a leading role in both. No other city attracted so much talent, so many geniuses. Berlin was long home to most, as well as to the greatest, German poets and thinkers, architects and sculptors, directors and stars of the stage, inventors and technical designers. On the other hand, however, Berlin produced the worst militarists and tolerated the world's worst criminals in its governments.' – from **That's Berlin** *(Berliner Zeitung, 1992)*

Checkpoint Charlie was the most famous crossing point between East and West Berlin. Most visitors to East Berlin from the West were only allowed in on a day visa and had to leave by midnight. Western visitors were required to exchange a certain amount of their 'hard' Western currency for GDR money.

THE BERLIN WALL

Today it is difficult to imagine what the Wall was like. Almost 165 kilometres long and 4 metres high. it was made of concrete with a rounded top, to make climbing over mre difficult. On the East German side there were mines, watchtowers, and guards with machine-guns and dogs. The East German government described it as the 'anti-Fascist Defence Wall', but its main purpose was to stop East Germans leaving for the West. (There already was an impassable border between the rest of the GDR and West Germany.) Between 1949 and 1961, 230,000 people a year left the GDR. Many were skilled and educated; 74 per cent were under 45 and 50 per cent under 25.

For almost 20 years, from 1952 to 1971, the telephone lines between the two parts of Berlin were cut. There were several border crossing points along the Wall. However, while all West Berliners could visit East Berlin (after showing their passport and buying a fixed amount of East German currency), the only East Berliners allowed to cross to the West were pensioners and people on official business.

Looking east across Berlin. In the distance is the Tiergarten (Animal Garden), the large park in the centre of the city. Beyond it is the television tower, built by the East German government in the 1960s, from which there are spectacular views of Berlin.

TWO HALF-CITIES

After the Wall was built, East Germany enjoyed a new stability and the economy improved markedly. In part this was because economic planners could now count on their best workers staying in the country. Perhaps, too, the population as a whole knew it had no alternative but to make the best of the situation. East Berlin was not only the biggest city in East Germany, but also an industrial and cultural centre. Visitors came from East and West to the famous Brecht Theatre and the museums.

West Berlin was the biggest city in West Germany. It also had important industries, and during the 1980s developed as a centre for high technology. The Berlin Philharmonic Orchestra and the Schaubühne Theatre became world famous, and the city was host to the annual International Film Festival.

UNIFICATION

In 1990 Berlin became the capital of the new Federal Republic of Germany. The government will move there from Bonn, in former West Germany, in the late 1990s.

The Bundesbank building in Frankfurt. The bank plays a key role in managing the German economy. It is independent of the government but must support its general economic policy.

Immediately after unification there was euphoria in both parts of Berlin. This soon disappeared as East Berliners became worried about losing jobs and West Berliners were annoyed about the way their 'island' was being overrun by Western businessmen, East Germans and East Europeans. Berlin has become a magnet for people from poorer countries to the East; some are refugees, others are looking for work. Some West Berliners whisper half-jokingly, 'If only we could have the Wall back!'

Berlin is now the biggest city between Paris and Moscow and Germany's largest industrial centre.

DECENTRALIZATION

Even though Berlin is the capital again, many of the activities that in Britain are centred on London, and in France on Paris, in Germany are divided up among various towns. This decentralization has its roots in Germany's past, when it was a collection of states before unification in 1871. Hamburg is a media centre: the influential weekly publications *Die Zeit*, *Der Spiegel* and *Stern* are published there, as is the daily paper *Bild*. Frankfurt is the financial capital: the Bundesbank, Germany's central bank, is based there, as are the headquarters of most leading banks and many insurance and advertising firms. Munich is the centre for fashion and, with Berlin, of the film industry. The German Confederation of Trade Unions is in Düsseldorf and the Employers' Federation in Cologne.

Industry

Germany is a leading industrial nation and has one of the highest standards of living in the world. It is the fifth largest consumer of energy.

Germany has few of its own raw materials and energy sources and so depends largely on imports. Though there are large deposits of coal, which will last for several decades, and the country provides about one-third of its own natural gas needs, there are few deposits of oil. Many minerals – for example copper, bauxite, manganese, phosphate and tin – which play a key role in industrial processes, also come from other countries.

The main coal reserves are in the Ruhr district in the central western part of the country and in the Saarland, which is slightly further south. These reserves total about 24 billion tonnes. There are also huge lignite, or browncoal, deposits – about 94 billion tonnes in all. Some of these are in the lower Rhine area in the west, but most are in the former GDR: in Brandenburg, Saxony, Saxony-Anhalt and the foothills of the Harz Mountains.

Germany also has many nuclear power stations, which account for about 38 per cent of the country's power supply. For many years there has been a lively debate in western Germany about their safety. Some people are afraid there could be an accident like the one in Chernobyl in the Ukraine in 1986.

NORTH SEA

BALTIC SEA

Hamburg

Hanover

Berlin

Elbe

Leipzig

Dresden

Cologne

Rhine

Frankfurt

Stuttgart

Danube

Munich

KEY

Gas

— Gas pipeline

Oil

····· Oil pipeline

Coal

△ Lead

◇ Lignite

○ Zinc

Mittelstand Firms

Mittelstand means a small or medium-sized business. Nine out of ten firms belong to this category. Today there are 1.2 million Mittelstand firms in western Germany and about 200,000 in eastern Germany, many of which are family-owned.

One reason for the development of Mittelstand firms is the federal structure of western Germany. Each Land has many small businesses and the regional government actively supports them. Around Stuttgart, the capital of Baden-Württemberg, for example, there are many firms that specialize in precision work. Some of them have been in existence for over a hundred years. A century ago the area was mainly poor agricultural land, frequently struck by famine. Many farmers emigrated, but some became watchmakers as a way of supplementing their income. As they developed a talent for precision work, many small firms specializing in woodwork, watchmaking, machine tools and other fields grew up. Some businesses became huge, like the car firm Daimler-Benz, which is now Germany's biggest company. But others have remained small, basing their success on specialization.

Mittelstand firms are particularly successful when they fill a gap in the market. Brita, a firm near Frankfurt, manufactures water filters for household use. Back in 1969, Heinz Hankammer was laughed at when he produced the first water filter, but he stuck with his idea and over the years built up a network of dealers in Germany. Today Brita is still successful because Hankammer knows almost all his employees personally and looks after them well. He provides a kindergarten for their children and a pension plan for when they retire.

A radio transmitter in Raisting, Bavaria, built and operated by TELEKOM, the telecommunications arm of the German postal service.

Much of Germany's economic strength is based on its manufacturing industry. The most important sectors are vehicle manufacture, chemicals, mechanical engineering, electrical engineering and aerospace. Traditional sectors like textiles and steel production have been in decline for some time.

NUMBER OF WORKERS BEFORE UNIFICATION	
EAST GERMANY	
Manufacturing, mining & utilites	3,500,000
Trade	869,000
Agriculture and Forestry	922,000
Construction	578,000
Transport & communication	630,000
Community, government & personal services	2,041,000
WEST GERMANY	
Manufacturing, mining & utilities	9,140,000
Trade	4,176,000
Agriculture, forestry & fishing	1,352,000
Construction	1,774,000
Transportation & communication	1,590,000
Community government & personal services	7,584,000

In western Germany alone there are 46,700 businesses. Only about 2 per cent of these are large companies with more than 1,000 employees. Most belong to the Mittelstand (see box). The large companies, though few in number, employ a large number of people – about half of the roughly 7 million people in industry. Together, they account

A lignite mine in Garzweiler, North Rhine Westphalia. Lignite mines are shallow (open-cast) and cheaper than deep mines, and lay waste huge tracts of land.

'In meeting the high-tech challenge to Europe, Germany has to play a key role. Together with France it must become the driving force within the European Community for mobilizing Europe's resources in a grand catching-up strategy and for leading Europe's societies and economies into the information age.' – **Konrad Seitz in Meet United Germany (Atlantik Brucke/FAZ Information Services, 1991)**

Trade Unions

Trade unions have played an important part in Germany's industrial development since the Second World War. Their relationship with employers has generally been cooperative rather than confrontational. One reason for this is that there are strict laws about when strikes may be called.

While Britain has some 300 unions, there are only 16 in the German Confederation of Trade Unions. They are organized on the principle of 'one industry, one union', which means that everybody who works in a particular industry belongs to the same union. So, for example, all the employees at Bosch (a large electrical engineering firm in Stuttgart), from mechanics to computer programmers, belong to the metalworkers' union. This makes the unions stronger as there are no disputes between unions in one firm, as has often been the case in Britain.

By law, most employees have some say in how a business is run. For example, in every firm employing five people or more, the management must agree to the setting up of a *Betriebsrat*, or works council, even where there is no union. The Betriebsrat is consulted on economic matters and has a say in deciding about working conditions, hiring and firing, plant closures and when holidays are taken. All large firms also have an *Aufsichtstrat*, or supervisory council, half of whose members are elected by the staff. Of course, managers are not always happy that their employees can influence company policy!

Members of the postal workers union (part of the German Confederation of Trade Unions) on strike. There has been an increase in the number of strikes in western Germany since unification.

Case Study: Volkswagen

German cars are famous around the world, and some of the best known are produced by Volkswagen. Volkswagen is Germany's second largest firm in terms of turnover and one of the four largest vehicle manufacturers in the world. The company was founded by Adolf Hitler in 1938 to produce a cheap 'people's car' and for forty years the 'Beetle' was Volkswagen's most famous product. It is still being produced in Brazil by a subsidiary of VW.

The Beetle, cheap, small and sturdy, was for many years the symbol of Volkswagen.

Volkswagen dominates the German market in smaller cars. Today the Golf, the most popular small car in Europe, is the company's best selling car.

Volkswagen has six factories in western Germany. The largest is in Wolfsburg in Lower Saxony, a town of 130,000 people that was built for and by Volkswagen. There is a saying that nothing can be done in Germany without Volkswagen and certainly not in Lower Saxony, where the firm is the single largest employer.

Volkswagen also owns the firm Audi, who make the smarter and more expensive Quattro and have become the third largest European exporter of luxury cars to the United States. Volkswagen has subsidiaries all around the world: in Spain, the Czech and Slovak republics, Brazil, Mexico, Argentina, Nigeria and China. Since unification Volkswagen has been investing more heavily than other German car firms in eastern Germany. The old East German car manufacturers collapsed in the face of competition from the west. Since 1991 a new factory at Mosel has been producing Golfs.

INDUSTRY'S SHARE OF GDP (1990)	
Germany:	39.4%
Japan:	34.1%
USA:	33.0%
UK:	30.0%
France:	28.6%

for about 50 per cent of total industrial turnover. Many of the companies are well known abroad: for example, Volkswagen, BMW and Daimler-Benz. Germany is the largest producers of cars in the world after Japan and the United States.

Structural change in the economy has meant that industry has declined in recent years. In western Germany, the contribution of industry to the Gross Domestic Product (the value of all goods and services produced in the course of a year) fell from 48.7 per cent in 1973 to 39.4 per cent in 1990.

A power station in Saxony, eastern Germany. By the end of the 1980s, East Germany provided about 75 per cent of its primary energy requirements from its own resources.

The leading industries of the future are in high technology. One of the biggest challenges facing German industry today is the need to develop a high technology to produce computers, consumer electronics (video recorders, CD players) and robots. The top high technology firms are Japanese and American – in computers, for example, American products dominate the German market. Without such an industry Germany could lose its position as one of the leading industrial nations in the world.

EXPORTS AND IMPORTS

Main exports: Motor vehicles, machinery, chemical products, electrical engineering goods, textiles and clothes.

Main imports: Electrical engineering goods, chemical products, motor vehicles, textiles and clothes, machinery, food and drink, raw materials, agricultural goods.

25

Industrial Pollution

Many Germans feel very strongly about pollution, whether it is caused by factories, cars or power stations, and there have often been heated debates on the subject.

Environmental organizations have often criticized BASF, one of Europe's biggest chemical firms, for dumping poisonous chemicals into the Rhine and polluting the air around Ludwigshafen. One German magazine accused BASF of using the river as a 'garbage chute' for carrying the company's rubbish into the North Sea.

Pollution in eastern Germany is an even bigger problem, and much of it has been caused by the chemical industry. In the town of Bitterfeld, for example, there were a lot of chemical factories. Before unification it was so badly polluted that, if United Nations standards had been applied, people would not have been allowed to live there. One of the first things a visitor would notice was the bitter smell in the air. The dirtiest chemical factories have been shut down since unification, but there are still millions of square metres of contaminated ground, which might take decades to clean up.

Before 1989, chemical

Germany has relatively strict laws controlling industrial emission, but problems remain. Sulphur dioxide emissions from lignite burning have been a major cause of pollution, particularly in eastern Germany.

enterprises produced about one-fifth of East Germany's Gross Domestic Product. Since unification they have been exposed to global competition and have suffered badly - not just because pollution means many have to be closed down, but also because they were over-staffed and produced goods that were too expensive. In the major centres of Bitterfeld, Halle, Leuna and Buna, about 50,000 of a total of 74,000 work places are expected to disappear.

Agriculture, Forestry and Fishing

About half of Germany's total area is given over to farming. Many German farms are highly mechanized and very productive, but Germany is not a country dominated by medium-sized or large farms, as are Britain, the USA or Australia. On the contrary, most farms are family farms and over 90 per cent are smaller than 50 hectares. There are big regional variations in the size and wealth of farms. In the north, in the states of North Rhine-Westphalia, Schleswig-Holstein and Lower Saxony, for example, farms are large and prosperous. There are some like this in Bavaria in the south, too, but on average southern farms are smaller than those in the north. German farmers, like their counterparts in other European countries, receive large subsidies from the European Union.

An unusual feature of German agriculture is the fact that almost half the farms, and the majority of really small ones, are run part-time by people whose main family income comes from another job. If one

27

partner has a full-time job elsewhere, for example, the other will work the farm and the wage earner will help in their spare time. So a worker at the electrical engineering firm Bosch in Stuttgart may go home after work and milk the cows.

The biggest-earning products of Germany's farms are milk, pork and beef, cereals and sugarbeet. Different regions are suitable for different types of farming: there are big grain farms on the north German Plain, in Lower Saxony and Schleswig-Holstein, and dairy farms in the hillier and mountainous areas of Bavaria. There are many pig farms in the north and west of the country, for example in North Rhine Westphalia. In some regions wine, fruit and vegetables are important. The grapes for Germany's famous wines are grown in the vineyards that line the banks of the rivers Rhine, Neckar, Moselle, and Main.

Germany is self-sufficient in grains, sugar, butter, pork and beef and almost so in eggs. Most vegetables and fruit, however, have to be imported.

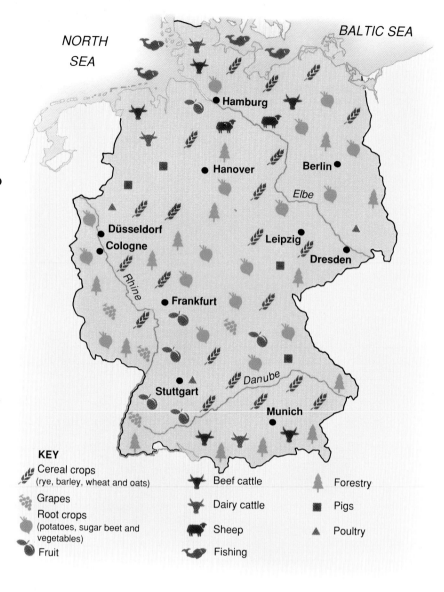

KEY

Cereal crops (rye, barley, wheat and oats)

Grapes

Root crops (potatoes, sugar beet and vegetables)

Fruit

Beef cattle

Dairy cattle

Sheep

Fishing

Forestry

Pigs

Poultry

FORESTRY

Almost one-third of Germany is covered by forest. The state with the largest forest area is Rhineland-Palatinate, that with the smallest (apart from the city-states) Schleswig-Holstein. These forests provide approximately 40 million cubic metres of timber every year, which meets about two-thirds of

Forestry is an important German industry. The damage to forests caused by pollution has been one reason for the rise and popularity of the Green Party.

domestic demand. Unfortunately, German forests have been badly hit by pollution from cars and factories, and only one-third are completely undamaged. Forests are not only an important national resource, they also play a big part in leisure and tourism, and Germans are worried about the threat to them.

In 1989 the fish catch was just over 400,000 tonnes. Government subsidies help keep the fishing fleet going.

FISHING

Germany has an extensive coastline in the north and fishing has long been an important industry there. German boats fish mainly in the North Sea, the Baltic Sea, in the Atlantic off Ireland and the United Kingdom, and around Greenland. But in all these areas there are many fewer fish than before and the size of Germany's fishing fleet has in recent years diminished considerably.

Beer

One of the most famous German products that uses agricultural produce is beer. Normally, the main ingredients are barley and hops, though wheat can also be used. Malt is the most important ingredient in beer, and 85 per cent of German beer is made with barley malt. The other 15 per cent is made with other malts.

Between 5,000 and 6,000 tons of hops are harvested each year. About 70 per cent are exported. The single largest area where hops are grown, and have been for over 500 years, is Hallertau.

Germans drink more beer than any other nation in the world – about 140 litres per person every year. And since not everyone drinks beer, some people drink a lot more than that! The production of German beer is regulated by a *Reinheitsgebot*, or beer purity regulation, passed by Duke Wilhelm IV of Bavaria in 1516. Wilhelm's decree, the oldest food law in the world that is still valid, stated that beer could only be brewed from barley, hops and water, but there have been some changes to the laws over the years.

A waitress carrying litre mugs (known as Steins) at the annual Munich Oktoberfest, the largest beer festival in the world.

In 1987 the European Court of Justice ruled that foreign breweries could import their beers to Germany, many of which are made with additives.

FACTS ABOUT BEER

There are 1,290 breweries in Germany, 121 in Belgium, 99 in the UK, 25 in France and 7 in Ireland. Eleven monasteries brew their own beer.

There are over 5,000 types of German beers.

Bavarians drink more beer than anyone else in Germany.

EASTERN GERMANY

Before German unification, the structure of farming in East Germany was very different to that of West Germany. East German farms were state-controlled and subsidized. They were also large: the average size of farms, or 'agricultural production cooperatives', was 1200 hectares.

By West European standards, East German agriculture was over-manned and highly inefficient. In 1990 restructuring, through privatization, of east German farms began and as a result output plummeted. Between 1989 and 1991, the agricultural labour force shrank from 850,000 to about 300,000. The area hardest hit was the northern Land of Mecklenburg-Western Pomerania, which accounted for almost 30 per cent of the former GDR's agricultural land.

Many agricultural workers in eastern Germany were reluctant to see agriculture privatized because they feared this would lead to unemployment.

Women weeding fields on a farm in eastern Germany. Today, eastern German farms are having to compete with more efficient western German and other West European farms.

AGRICULTURAL STATISTICS

Between 1973 and 1990 the contribution of agriculture, forestry and fishing to Germany's Gross Domestic Product declined from 3% to 1.6%. In Britain the figure for 1991 was 2.0%, in the USA 2.0%, in France 3.4% and in Japan 7.2%.

Agricultural productivity has increased. In 1950, in West Germany, one farm worker fed 10 people; today the figure (for the whole of Germany) is 75.

The number of farms has decreased. In 1950, in West Germany, there were about 1.6 million farms employing almost a quarter of the working population; today there are just under 600,000 farms. 2.8% of the working population (830,000 people) earns its living from them.

The average size of a farm is 20 hectares, compared with 30 in France and 70 in Britain. The largest farms are in Schleswig-Holstein (average 40 hectares) and the smallest in Baden-Württemberg (average 15 hectares).

Daily Life

There are hundreds of popular festivals every year in Germany. Here, a mountain of pretzels is on sale at the Museumsuferfest in Frankfurt.

Germany is one of the most densely populated countries in the world. About one in three Germans lives in one of the country's 85 cities (with populations of 100,000 or more). About half live in towns and only a small number in villages. Some parts of Germany are extremely crowded: 3.4 million live in Greater Berlin, for example, and experts predict it will be nearer 8 million by the year 2000. Other areas , such as the agricultural region of Mecklenburg-Western Pomerania and the moorlands of the North German Plain, are very thinly populated.

HOUSING

Most Germans live in flats. In western Germany there is a shortage of accommodation. One reason for this is that more and more people are living alone, so each individual needs his or her own flat. Another reason is the large number of ethnic Germans that have come to the country since 1988 from Russia, Romania and Poland. In 1990 about 400,000 arrived, and many had to be housed temporarily in camps, hostels or disused buildings while a crash housing programme was started.

In Western Germany, most flats are well-built and quite large. But rents are high, especially in the big cities, and quite a few people have to have their rents 'topped up' by the government. In eastern Germany, by contrast, quite a few flats are in bad condition and a lot of money has to be spent on renovating them (about 20 per cent have no bath or shower, for example). In the GDR rents were very low; they have shot up since unification and many people on low incomes cannot afford them.

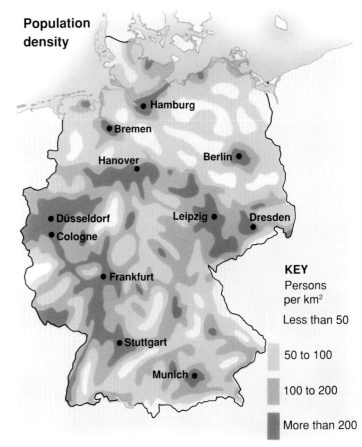

Population density

Hamburg

Bremen

Hanover

Berlin

Düsseldorf
Cologne

Leipzig

Dresden

Frankfurt

Stuttgart

Munich

KEY
Persons per km²

Less than 50

50 to 100

100 to 200

More than 200

FOOD AND SHOPPING

Two of the best-known German foods are bread and sausages. This may sound dull, but it isn't: there are some 200 different varieties of bread and almost as many kinds of *Wurst* (sausage). In the north, near the coast, a lot of fish is eaten. Different regions produce their own specialities. Hamburg is famous for its eel, plum and vegetable soup. Stuttgart calls itself the *Spätzle* capital – *Spätzle* are delicious small crinkly flour noodles that are served with meat dishes.

This butcher's shop displays some of the many types of meat available in Germany.

There are now many foreign food restaurants in Germany, some of them run by foreign workers. So in the big cities, at least, it is common to find Turkish, Greek, Italian and Spanish restaurants.

The western German diet has changed a lot in the last forty years as the standard of living has improved and people have become

33

more aware of healthy eating. Before the Second World War Germans ate nearly three times as many potatoes as the British; today they eat 30 per cent less. Consumption of vegetables, fruits and meat has almost doubled since the 1950s.

In the GDR fresh fruit and vegetables were not as readily available as in West Germany. Since unification east Germans have been eating much more of these than before.

A schoolgirl using a computer. Personal computers are increasingly used in schools, as well as on vocational training courses.

EDUCATION

School begins at 8 am in Germany. Pupils work right through to 1 pm, with only short breaks between lessons, and then go home for lunch. Once they have done their homework they have the afternoon free. Most small children attend kindergartens, which are run by local government, churches, associations, firms or private individuals. Because kindergartens are not part of the state education system, parents have to contribute to the cost.

Children start primary school when they are six and stay there for four years. The teachers then suggest to parents which secondary school would be best for their children: the *Hauptschule*, where children stay until they are fifteen; the *Realschule*, which pupils attend until they are sixteen; or the *Gymnasium*, which they attend for nine years. The first two years at this stage are called the *Orientierungsstufe*, or orientation phase, which is a period when children and parents can revise their choice of school. Some Länder have replaced the three different types of schools with the *Gesamtschule*, or comprehensive school.

Most *Hauptschule* pupils go on to a vocational training course, which is essential for many occupations. *Realschule* pupils get an intermediate certificate between *Hauptschule* and *Gymnasium*, which allows them to attend a *Fachschule*, or technical school, a specialized school that offers vocational training. Pupils who want to go on to university have to take an exam called the *Abitur* at the *Gymnasium*.

LEISURE

More Germans travel abroad each year as tourists than the citizens of any other country – even than those of the United States, whose population is three times larger. For eastern Germans, travel to the west was particularly popular after the Wall came down. This is not surprising, because for decades most of them had been able to travel west only in exceptional circumstances. But many eastern Germans continue to holiday in the cheaper countries of eastern Europe, such as Romania.

Italy, Austria, Spain and the United States are favourite holiday destinations, though many Germans take holidays at home in the North Sea and Baltic Sea resorts or in the picturesque Black Forest and Harz Mountains.

Every year hundreds of thousands of people take part in pre-Lenten carnivals, called *Fasching* or *Karneval*. Most of these take place in the Catholic parts of the country in the south, such as the Rhineland and Bavaria. The biggest

The Alps, the Harz Mountains and the Black Forest are popular areas for camping. German campsites have facilities of a very high standard.

Tourists on the Canary Islands, off the north-west coast of Africa. Popular European resorts cater for the German package tourist, offering German drink, food and atmosphere.

'With rucksacks and strong shoes, and maybe in lederhosen too, parties of Germans young and old go hiking and camping in the wide woodlands, where you never see a 'Keep out' sign, for by law even privately owned forests are freely open to all.' – John Ardagh, Germany and the Germans (Penguin Books, 1991)

35

carnival of all is in Cologne, where the high point is the famous Rose Monday procession, when a million people line the streets to watch floats with huge caricatures of politicians and people dressed in comic uniforms.

MEDIA

There are about 410 newspapers in Germany, most of them local and regional. They cover the whole political spectrum, from the small left-wing *tageszeitung*, produced in Berlin, to the right-wing *Bild*. *Bild*, a popular tabloid newspaper, sells 4.5 million copies each day!

Hamburg is a media centre: the influential weekly publications Die Zeit, Der Spiegel, and Stern are published there, as is the daily paper Bild.

The weekly magazine *Der Spiegel*, which sells over 1 million copies, has a reputation for investigating and uncovering scandals in all parts of the political spectrum. In 1984, for example, it helped reveal that all the political parties except the Greens had been taking bribes from the huge Flick financial group.

There are three main TV channels, one produced by ZDF in Mainz, the other two by ARD. ARD is actually a network of 11 regional broadcasting corporations, each of which produces some programmes for a local audience and the rest for the network – which means that an evening's viewing can hop from, say, Hamburg to Frankfurt to Munich. Many programmes are taken from American television, though of course they have to be dubbed.

There are a lot of documentaries, news broadcasts, cultural programmes and commentaries on German TV. There is some advertising, though ARD and ZDF get most of their money from licence fees. Advertisements may only be shown for 20 minutes a day between 6 pm and 8 pm!

Private TV stations are increasingly popular. They show mainly sport, Hollywood films and old American sitcoms, but they also broadcast some hard-hitting news programmes, some of them presented by publications such as *Der Spiegel.*

TRANSPORT

In Germany, the private car is the most popular means of transport. Today there are more cars than ever on German roads - about 45 million in all. More freight is transported by trucks than by rail or in ships.

There is a total of 221,000 km of trunk roads in Germany, including 11,000 km of motorway. Only the USA has more kilometres of truck road. German *Autobahnen* (motorways)

An InterCity Express near Gelnhausen in Hesse. Introduced in 1991, the ICE can travel at up to 250 km/hour.

A Lufthansa jumbo jet at Frankfurt airport. Lufthansa was founded in 1926 to provide regular passenger services throughout Europe. By 1938 Lufthansa offered a non-stop passenger service from Berlin to New York. Since the re-establishment of German commercial aviation in the mid-1950s, Lufthansa has become a leading international airline.

In 1991, 1,530 million passengers travelled a total of 57,034,000 kilometres on German railways.

Germany's first train service, covering the 5 kilometres between Nuremberg and Furth in Bavaria, opened in 1835.

Today, Germany has 44,080 kilometres of railway line.

Inland Waterways (1990)

	Length of waterways in use (km)	No of goods vessels	Tonnes carried (millions)
Germany	6,700	3,564	310.1
France	5,023	4,565	56.8
Netherlands	4,831	3,019	240.6
Belgium	1,514	2,214	90.9

not only connect northern and southern Europe, they will soon be linking East and West, as millions of Deutschmarks are being invested in motorways between western and eastern Germany. Unfortunately, in former East Germany, where people have had to adjust to a sudden increase in traffic and faster cars, there has been a sharp rise in road accidents.

Cars and trucks are one of the main sources of air pollution and many cities have well-developed rail networks which they encourage commuters and other travellers to use. The New InterCity Express (ICE) high-speed trains link various cities, for example Stuttgart and Mannheim.

Rivers and canals are important transport routes, and inland shipping accounts for about 20 per cent of total freight traffic. Every year, some 3,900 ships use the 6,700 km of

The container port on the Elbe river in Hamburg is the world's seventh largest. Hamburg's port is the easternmost European port in the North Sea. The North Sea-Baltic Sea canal connects it with the Baltic Sea.

navigable inland waterways, for example the Rhine and the Elbe rivers.

Over 80 million people use Germany's airports each year. Many of them go through the airport at Frankfurt-am-Main, one of Europe's busiest.

SOCIAL SECURITY

Germany has one of the most comprehensive and generous social security systems in the world. It is funded out of the contributions made by employers, employees and the government.

The central pillar of the system is the pensions scheme, which pays old-age and invalidity pensions. The money for old-age pensions comes from the contributions paid by people currently in work. Because the proportion of elderly people is growing, there is some doubt whether in the near future there will be enough money to pay these pensions.

Everyone is required to make regular payments to a health insurance scheme, and they are then entitled to free health care. Doctors are very well paid. Today, western Germany has one of the world's highest doctor/population ratios: 3 per 1,000, compared with 1.7 per 1,000 in Britain and 1.8 in the United States.

One of the most popular forms of medical treatment is the *Kur*, or health cure. Patients are sent to stay for a month or so at a spa specializing in their particular complaint, where they drink the local mineral waters. Up to 6 million people a year attend spas, many of them paid for by the social security system.

The social security system is now very expensive: in 1991 it cost DM 12,000 per inhabitant. Since unification the social security system covers the 16 million new citizens. However, because the eastern German economy is still very weak, the eastern part of the country is unable to finance much of these social security payments itself. As a result, the German government has to raise taxes and borrow money to cover the costs of the system.

An open-air swimming pool at a health spa in Bad Waldliesborn in western Germany. In the hilly parts of central and southern Germany there are over 200 health spas.

Foreigners in Germany

There are almost 6 million foreigners in Germany, of whom about 1 million are refugees. The rest are workers and their families. Foreign workers first came to West Germany in the 1950s, when the booming economy needed extra labour. They were called *Gastarbeiter* (guest workers), because at first they came only for a short period. Now about 60 per cent of the foreign population has been in Germany for 10 years or more.

About one-third are Turkish and there are many from former Yugoslavia, Italy and Greece.

Foreign workers have found integration into German society difficult. They are often the target of racist behaviour, particularly when unemployment is high – though joblessness tends to be almost twice as high among foreign workers as among Germans. There as been a big increase in racist attacks on foreigners, both workers and refugees, since unification, and some of these attacks have been fatal. But there have also been many anti-racist rallies, as in December 1992, when 300,000 people demonstrated in Hamburg.

Turkish women in the Kreuzberg district in the middle of Berlin. This is the biggest Turkish community outside Turkey.

'I get on well with the Germans and I like living here. My main problems are legal and political, for neither government makes things easy . . . Germany won't grant me citizenship unless I give up my Turkish passport, and Turkey won't let me take that step legally unless I first do my military service – and I hate the thought of 22 tough months in the Army under that harsh regime . . . But it's hard to find a job here as a non-EEC foreigner. I have no legal security, but I love Germany.' **– Turk, 25, former student living in Mainz.**

RELIGION

About 58 million Germans belong to a Christian Church, though many fewer actually go to church. Roughly 30 million are Protestants, about 28 million are Roman Catholics, and a minority belong to other Churches. Members pay a tax to their Church, which means the Churches are well-off. (If someone wants to resign from a Church they have to make a special declaration to a state authority.) The Churches run nursery schools, hospitals, old people's and nursing homes, and training centres. They also send a lot of money to the Third World, for example to finance famine relief in Ethiopia.

The Churches are very involved in public life and in politics. In the 1960s, for example, the West German Protestant Churches helped lay the ground for Willy Brandt's Ostpolitik, by urging better relations with Poland and a gentler attitude to East Germany. And in the 1980s many Protestants became involved in the huge West German peace movement; priests, and even some bishops, spoke out against nuclear weapons.

In the GDR the Protestant Church was the biggest Church. In the 1980s it provided protection and meeting-rooms for independent peace, human rights and ecology activists, many of whom played leading roles in the peaceful revolution of 1989. Today, however, the Church is adjusting to a smaller political role.

After Christianity, the biggest religion in Germany is Islam. There are about 1.7 million Muslims, most of whom are people from Turkey.

St Michael's Protestant church in Hamburg was built in the eighteenth century in the Baroque style. It was destroyed by fire in 1806, rebuilt, destroyed again in the Second World War and restored after the war. Although most Germans are Christians, there are also Muslims and others.

42

Facing the Future

East German Trabants and Volkswagen Polos being assembled in Zwickau, east Germany. Volkswagen has three factories in the former GDR.

One of the most challenging tasks facing Germany in the 1990s is the integration of west and east.

At the end of 1989 and the beginning of 1990 thousands of East Germans were crossing to the West, at times as many as 2,000 per day, in search of a better standard of living. The West German government under Chancellor Kohl argued that the best way to put a stop to this was to rebuild the inefficient East German economy to the West German standard - to replace the centralized economic system with a market economy. To do this, the government said, the GDR and West Germany would have to be unified as soon as possible. The great majority of East Germans and most West Germans agreed. On 3 October 1990 the two countries were unified.

The dismantling of the old economic system has caused the collapse of east German industry and agriculture. The result has been massive unemployment and insecurity. This collapse happened partly because the east German economy was much weaker than the west German: for example, products were of a lower quality, many enterprises were run down, and roads, railways and telephone lines were in a decrepit state. For this reason Western firms have been slower to invest in eastern Germany than was predicted. Another reason is that unification took place too quickly – the east German economy was not given time to adapt to difficult new conditions. At the

East Germans window-shopping in Berlin shortly after the Wall was opened. Initial enthusiasm for West German goods has in part given way to a nostalgia for traditional East German products.

43

Women and Unification

In eastern Germany, women have been particularly badly hit by unemployment, especially in traditionally 'female' branches of the economy such as textiles, chemicals, light industry and electrical engineering. One textile enterprise, the Saxon Cotton and Thread Spinning Works, used to employ 13,000 workers and its products were exported to over thirty countries. By 1992 production had been fallen and the workforce had shrunk to 1,300.

Many people in eastern Germany, perhaps as many as half, are living on the poverty line. Poverty affects single parents, almost all of whom are women, particularly badly. In the GDR, the state supported single mothers: they could rely on having a job and a kindergarten at work for the children. This support has decreased markedly in united Germany. One mother, Ute Pust, went back to her job in a hotel kitchen after taking maternity

In the GDR, women could rely on the state providing care for their children while they were at work.

leave, a break from work to allow her to look after her new baby. In the GDR she would have been able to go back to her old job, but her new employer said simply, 'Either you work on the late shift, or not at all.'

In the GDR about 90 per cent of women between the ages of sixteen and sixty either had a job or were engaged in some form of training (compared with 63 per cent in West Germany). Most of them had to do the bulk of household work and looked after the children too – what is known as the 'double burden'. Yet many valued the economic independence and the social life work brought them. In united Germany it looks as if women will be under pressure to leave paid work to men and stay at home.

The flags of the member countries of the European Union (EU) and the EU flag. Germany and France are the two most influential members of the EU and want it to become stronger and more united.

same time, the economies of other formerly communist countries in Eastern Europe – Russia, Poland, and Hungary, for example – have been undergoing similar changes, which means that the traditional markets for East German goods have disappeared. Throughout eastern Germany businesses have been closing down. A team of US economists has called it 'one of the worst and sharpest economic depressions in European history'.

Unification has also revealed, and partly created, a big gap in outlook between east and west Germans. East German enthusiasm for unification in 1989 and 1990 has lessened as unemployment and insecurity have risen. Many feel that their country has been taken over by western Germany and that west Germans treat them like second-class citizens because they are poorer and lived for forty years under communism.

Many west Germans, on the other hand, resent that so much taxpayers' money is being spent on eastern Germany. The German government is transferring billions of Deutschmarks of subsidies to the east – between DM 80 and DM 100 billion per year. West Germans are particularly angry because the western German economy is itself in trouble, with unemployment climbing steadily. They feel their money is going to the east when it should be spent in western Germany.

The Berlin Wall may have come down, it is said, but there is still a wall in people's heads. It will be a long time before the two parts of Germany have become completely united.

'The real task of combining and interweaving two such unlikely societies and economies still lies ahead. So disparate in appearance, attitude, economic prowess and recent history are East and West Germany that one cannot ignore the high degree of artificiality of some aspects of unification. "A collision under one roof" was how one observer described it.' – **Thomas Kielinger in Meet United Germany** *(Atlantik Brücke/FAZ Information Services, 1991)*

Glossary

Chancellor   The German equivalent of prime minister.

Cold War   The state of strained relations between the United States (and other Western countries) and the Soviet Union (and other East European countries) that lasted from 1945 to 1989.

Coalition   A union or alliance (particularly of political parties or states).

COMECON   The Council for Mutual Economic Assistance. An organization established in 1949 for improving trade between the Soviet Union and other East European states. It was dissolved in 1991.

Communism   The view put forward by Karl Marx that private wealth should be abolished and held in common. In practice a system of government under which industry and commerce are controlled by the state.

European Union   Formerly the European Community (EC) or European Economic Community (EEC). An association within which 12 European states (Belgium, Denmark, France, Germany, Greece, Ireland, Italy, Luxembourg, Netherlands, Spain, Turkey, the United Kingdom) cooperate increasingly closely on economic, social and political affairs.

Federal   Relating to a union of states or nations (or, in the case of Germany, of Länder) which run their own domestic affairs, but act together in affairs of national or international importance.

Free Democratic Party (FDP)   Small, centrist German political party that has held the balance of power in most post-Second World War German governments.

First World War   Fought from 1914 to 1918, this was the first of the two great European wars in the twentieth century. The Allies (Britain, France, Russia and, later, Italy and the United States) fought, and defeated, the Central Powers (Germany, Austria-Hungary and the Turkish empire).

Gross Domestic Product (GDP)   The total manufactured goods (cars, ships, computers, etc) and services produced by an economy in a given period, usually one year.

Land (plural **Länder**)   The German word for the individual states (16 in all) that make up Germany. Each Land has considerable decision-making powers of its own.

Market economy   The economic system in which all or most businesses are owned privately, and the forces of supply and demand operate unhampered by government regulation or other interference.

North Atlantic Treaty Organization (NATO)   The Western military alliance, set up in 1949. Its members are Belgium, Canada, Denmark, France, Germany, Greece, Iceland, Italy, Netherlands, Norway, Portugal, Turkey, the United Kingdom and the United States.

Ostpolitik   The policy pursued by Willy Brandt, West German chancellor from 1969 to 1974, which aimed at improving relations with the Soviet Union, East Germany and other states in Eastern Europe.

Pension   Money paid regularly to a person for past services or on retirement.

Second World War   Fought from 1939 to 1945, the second major European war of the century. The Allies (the United States, The Soviet Union, Britain, France, Australia, New Zealand and others) defeated the Axis powers (Germany, Italy and Japan).

Services   Producer goods which are mainly intangible and are often consumed at the same time as they are produced – for example, the services of an orchestra or a teacher.

Social Democratic Party (SDP)   One of Germany's two biggest political parties (the other is the centre-right Christian Democratic Union), the SDP is a centre-left party.

Subsidies Money paid by a government to help an industry, service or region of a country because such aid is in the interests of the general public.

Turnover The total income from sales of a business.

United Nations An international organization whose purpose is to foster cooperation amongst its member countries. The UN was founded in 1945.

Warsaw Pact Properly known as the Warsaw Treaty Organization, the Warsaw Pact (founded in 1955) was a military alliance of the countries of Eastern Europe. Its members were Albania (until 1968), Czechoslovakia, East Germany, Hungary, Poland, Romania and the Soviet Union. The Warsaw Pact was wound up in 1991.

Weimar Republic Germany's first democratic republic, from 1919 to 1933.

Further information

German embassies have an information section for enquiries about Germany and will be able to provide a useful booklet. Your local library will have a yearbook that contains a lot of basic information about Germany. Goethe Institute libraries are an excellent source of information. They stock newspapers, magazines, books, slide sets and audio-visual cassettes. They also run German courses at all levels. National tourist offices are usually a good source of leaflets and posters.

Books to read

Germany by Charlotte Drews-Bernstein and Dan Garrett (Heinemann, 1991)

Germany by David Flint (Simon & Schuster, 1992)

Germany and the Germans by Anita Ganeri (Gloucester Press, 1992)

Germany: the Reunification of a Nation by Catherine and John Bradley (Gloucester Press, 1992)

Living in Berlin by Barbara Einhorn (Macdonald, 1986) A useful picture of life in Berlin before the wall came down.

The New Europe – Maastricht and Beyond by Elizabeth Roberts (Watts Books, 1994)

The Rhine by Mark Smalley (Wayland, 1992)

West German Food and Drink by Barbara Einhorn (Wayland, 1988)

PICTURE ACKNOWLEDGEMENTS
The publisher wishes to thank the following for supplying photographs for use as illustrations in this book: Camera Press 10, 12; Eye Ubiquitous 4, 14, 17, 31, 35 (below), 36, 42, 43 (below); Hutchison Library 44; Robert Harding 21, 27 (top), 38, 40; M. Kerr 35; J. Rowe 24; Tony Stone 3, 6, 15 (top), 27 (below), 39; Topham Picture Library 8, 13, 23, 25, 29, 30, 41; Trip 32, 43 (top), 45; Wayland Picture Library 7, 9, 15 (bottom), 29(inset); ZEFA 16, 19, 22, 26, 29 (top), 33, 34, 37.
Maps were provided by Peter Bull.

Index

The figures in **bold** refer to photographs and maps.